I Send My Child To School, What More Do You Want?

Regenia M. Rawlinson

To my husband David, my best friend and strongest advocate, and my three wonderful children David, Bradford, and Brittany, my inspiration and joy. I am proud of them.

CONTENTS

INTRODUCTION

Bobby's and Kevin's parents provide two compelling examples of what happens when parents are involved. Bobby was a ninth grade student whose parents made sure he always had his homework and was ready for class. They called the school regularly to check on his attendance and chat with his teachers about his progress. If Bobby needed extra help, they made sure he showed up for after school tutoring. Kevin was number one in a class of 514. From kindergarten, his mother and father attended most parent meetings; one was present at every award ceremony, traveled with him to band competitions, financed summer camps, and conferred regularly with his teachers.

Not all children with parents like Kevin's are number one in their class, but they generally do well in school. My experience over the last thirty-plus years shows me a direct correlation between student achievement and parental involvement. Students perform well in school when their parents are involved in their education. Many parents like Kevin's review report cards, volunteer at the school, monitor completion of assignments, and join parent organizations to foster achievement. The impact of parental involvement is evident in higher test scores, increased grade point averages, access to scholarships, and successful college admissions.

Since parental involvement promotes students success in school, why do we not focus more on how to involve parents in certification programs? When I earned degrees in special education and in guidance and counseling, discussions of parental involvement were brief and general. I speculated that we did not talk extensively about parental involvement because our professors assumed that we, as teachers, would naturally know how to involve parents. Some teachers do know, but many do not. In my current position as a school counselor and director of school counseling, I consult with teachers regularly about parental involvement. They ask me what they can do to encourage parents to attend parent-teacher conferences, ask students for report cards, sign important forms, or attend open house.

Training clearly helps teachers and other educators acquire invaluable knowledge about involving parents. I surveyed over a hundred teachers about the training they received for involving parents in their teacher education programs. Some attended colleges and universities in their own state and many out-of-state. Overwhelmingly, middle and high school teachers had no courses and did not mention parental involvement on their syllabus. They did not have speakers and had not researched ways to work with the parents of the students they teach. Some elementary teachers indicated that they had limited discussions of parental involvement in some of their courses. Three elementary teachers recalled a speaker giving a presentation on effective means of communicating with parents where the speaker discussed things such as sending weekly notes home, calling parents at night, and inviting parents to visit the classroom.

Offering pre-service training to individuals enrolled in certification programs will help them acquire the skills needed to work with parents effectively. They learn what do to gain parents' support. Assuming they naturally know how to involve parents likely puts some students' academic achievement at risk.

Involving parents appropriately means educators must understand how parents want and need to be involved. Some parents request a parent conference each grading period. Some parents are satisfied with periodic progress reports from teachers. Others want to be notified every time their child fails to complete an assignment or misbehaves in class. Still others expect teachers to send written reports home daily or weekly. Many parents attend every open house, while others attend only if they feel the need. Some parents see volunteering to help in the classroom as appropriate involvement. Contributing items to fund-raising efforts or helping their children sell cookies or fruit to the neighbors is involvement enough for some.

Some parents have unique barriers that prevent them from attending school functions or understanding written information. The barriers parents face must be considered when teachers invite them to participate in their children's education in ways crafted by educators. Understanding the barriers parents face is one among many positive attributes a teacher needs for successful parental involvement. Educators must guard against letting their personal beliefs or assumptions prevent them from using a variety of methods to involve parents. They must also be cautious not to assume that parental involvement means the same thing to all parents.

Increasing parental involvement in childhood education is a central theme in the discussion about improving the educational system. If student achievement increases when parents are involved, the need for parental involvement is compelling. Every year, parental involvement was among the top priorities at the school and in the school district where I worked. District administrators saw that faculty and staff needed to develop skills for involving parents in childhood education. To that end they provided professional development opportunities for faculty and staff to learn more about increasing parental involvement. They found that parental involvement is directly correlated with student achievement.

At educational conferences I attend, educators from across the nation talk about the importance of parental involvement and the strategies they use to involve parents. It appears that, like my district, other districts across the nation are taking aggressive steps to increase parental involvement.

The title of this manual is the result of an incident involving a student and a parent. The principal called the parent because her son, Sam, had been referred seven times for failure to complete work. The teacher wrote notes to the parents the first two times Sam refused to work. The parents did not respond. The third time she referred Sam to the principal for discipline. His work habits did not improve. Upon Sam's seventh referral, the principal called the parents and insisted they come for a conference with him and the school counselor— yours truly. The mother was obviously agitated throughout the conference. She shifted in her seat often, was non-responsive, her arms stubbornly folded until the end of the conference. When the principal asked her for suggestions to encourage Sam to complete his work, she stood up and said, *"I send my child to school! What more do you want?* I punish him at home when he misbehaves, and I expect you to discipline him at school when he refuses to work." She picked up her purse and walked out of the principal's office. For her, a conference was not what she wanted or felt she needed. Discipline was the school's responsibility when Sam was there and hers when he was at home.

"*What more do you want?*" is a question teachers and educators must answer. Knowing how to respond can make the difference in gaining parents' support or alienating them. This manual hopes to help teachers and educators respond to the question in ways that will win parents over and increase their confidence.

I have attended state and national events for educators where parental involvement was a recurring theme. Most recently I participated in a leadership conference sponsored by the South Carolina Department of Education (SDE) and the South Carolina Association of School Administrators (SCASA). Among the more than a thousand who attended were principals, assistant principals, deans, curriculum coordinators, and district office personnel. Whether the focus in a session was changing school climate or raising test scores, parental involvement was mentioned as a key factor in getting results. Presenters and participants agreed that though parental involvement differs from elementary schools to secondary schools, all schools need parental involvement to foster academic achievement. They also agreed that teachers and other educators need more training on ways to involve parents meaningfully.

Parental involvement training for teachers and educators can be done a number of ways. One is to give teachers books on parental involvement to read and discuss in groups. *I Send My Child to School! What More Do You Want?* can help educators involve parents in their children's education meaningfully. The book covers four areas: 1) **Awareness,** 2) **Strategies,** 3) **Implementation,** and 4) **Assessment**. Awareness, strategy, implementation, and assessment are essential to staying focused on parental involvement. Part 1, *Awareness,* explores personal assumptions, beliefs, barriers, benefits, responsibilities, and parental attributes, as well as the impact of parental involvement. Part 2, *Strategies,* includes specific techniques teachers can use to involve parents of various socio-economic backgrounds. Part 3, *Implementation,* summarizes key elements for involving parents successfully in their children's education. Part 4, *Assessment,* reviews traditional and nontraditional forms of parental involvement.

One more thing. Parental involvement affects the entire school community and affects the success of the educational process profoundly. Principals, teachers, curriculum coordinators, hall monitors, teaching assistants, counselors, and assistant principals all play a role in educating children. Throughout this manual, I refer to teachers, educators, or teachers and other educators. When

I refer specifically to the classroom, I say *teachers.* When I say *educators,* I include everybody. I believe everybody who works directly with children should read this manual.

Part One
Awareness

Wilbur was among the first group of special education students I taught. He came to school every day with offensive body odor, and the other children complained about it. He smiled and moved quietly about the classroom, completing all his assignments. He never retaliated or tried to explain why he smelled. He grew accustomed to teasing and unkind comments from the other students. I disciplined students promptly when they teased Wilbur. When I talked with him about the odor, he hung his head and said nothing. Day after day, Wilbur showed up for class that way. I concluded his parents could not care much about him if they let him come to school with body odor.

After two months, I decided to make a home visit. I knocked at the door. Wilbur opened it and invited me in. Freshly laundered clothes lay on chairs, waiting to be put away. I stopped in the first room, which Wilbur called the living room. The house smelled the same way Wilbur did.

Wilbur told his mother I was in the living room to see her. She came in and invited me to sit down. *Where am I going to sit?* I asked myself. Clothes covered the chairs. She cleared a space large enough for me to sit on the sofa. After we exchanged pleasantries, I discussed Wilbur's body odor and how the other students teased him. She said the odor was the smell of kerosene. They used kerosene to heat their house, and the fumes left the house, clothes, and the people who lived there smelling like coal oil.

The smell of kerosene was unfamiliar to me and to some of my students. I was glad I visited Wilbur's home. I realized that his mother did care about him but was powerless do anything about the odor. I also understood why Wilbur did not retaliate. When warmer weather arrived, Wilbur no longer came to school with that odor.

Before I learned of Wilbur's situation, I made unfounded assumptions that could have prevented me from involving Wilbur's mother. Learning about Wilbur's situation helped me understand his circumstances. For the purpose of this manual, I define awareness as examining issues that encourage or discourage parental involvement. Some of those issues are:

- awareness of personal assumptions, belief systems, and prejudices that can affect relationships with family;
- awareness of barriers to family involvement;
- awareness of benefits of parental involvement;
- awareness of teacher attributes for successful parental involvement.

Awareness of Personal Assumptions, Belief Systems, and Prejudices

Awareness of personal assumptions, beliefs, and prejudices that can affect relationships with a family is important. If educators harbor feelings that damage relationships with parents, those feelings can prevent them from involving parents meaningfully. It is crucial that teachers be aware of their views of parents from different cultures, races, and socioeconomic backgrounds.

What educators believe about various ethnic groups greatly influences how they interact with parents. Schools are places of rich cultural diversity with various ethnic group increasing in numbers. Parents of all socio-economic groups need appropriate responses from teachers to encourage involvement. Teachers must therefore examine their own beliefs, prejudices, and views about the parents of the students they serve.

One way to examine beliefs and views about different cultures is self-reflection, a technique that requires people to think about their attitude toward interacting and working with people who are culturally different from them. The method helps teachers uncover negative feelings and assumptions which inhibit them from involving parents.

Awareness of Barriers to Parental Involvement

Developing a positive relationship with parents is difficult if educators do not understand the barriers or challenges parents face. Learning about them is probably one of the most important steps a teacher can take to build teacher-parent relationships. Samantha's parents often worked ten hour shifts and could attend parent meetings only in the evening. If they wanted to attend an event at the school, they had to depend on neighbors to drive them; they did not own a car. Long working hours and lack of transportation kept Samantha's parents from coming to school. Those are two common barriers to parental involvement. Schools must be aware of such barriers and work with parents to resolve them. Other barriers include:

- *Preparation.* Teachers and other educators must develop a well-organized plan for involving parents.
- *Shared understanding.* Culture, attitudes, and practices often dictate what parents see as appropriate involvement, which may differ from what educators see as suitable. Educators must understand the culture, background,

practices, and attitudes of the parents they serve.

- *Coaching.* Educators lack adequate training. Schools serious about involving parents can give teachers information about different ways to involve parents and help them understand the barriers that keep parents from being more active.

- *Suitable parental involvement.* Many types of involvement may not be acceptable to both parents and educators. Some educators find they are comfortable with traditional family involvement activities, such as parents supporting school programs and attending school meetings. Some parents are more interested serving in an advisory capacity or advocating for programmatic changes than in other types of parental involvement. Competing and conflicting expectations can further inhibit strong home-school partnerships.

- *Negative attitudes.* Both teachers and parents often have negative attitudes toward parental involvement. Some educators believe some parents are neither interested in participating in their children's education nor qualified to do so. Many educators do not believe parents care about the education of their children.

- *Competing values.* Competing values further complicate parental involvement. As the population's ethnic diversity increases, educators and parents likely come from different cultural and economic backgrounds which can lead to competing values and beliefs.
- *Language and literacy barriers.* Some economically disadvantaged minority parents or non English-speaking parents face language and literacy barriers.
- *Neighborhood fears.* Parents may fear attending school events at night if they live in dangerous neighborhoods. Educators can help parents establish car pools or organize meetings at neighborhood centers that provide better levels of security so parents need not go far to obtain information from the teacher.
- *Time.* Often both parents work outside the home. Some single parents work two jobs.
- *Mistrust of the school system.* Some parents do not trust educators to treat their children fairly, possibly the result of how they were treated when they were in school. Some parents had unfavorable experiences in school and often associate school with hurt, shame, and failure. Or they may mistrust public education and public educators generally. Whatever

the reason, teachers must do what they can to gain the parents' trust. Trust creates the atmosphere in which teachers and parents can work cooperatively.

Awareness of the Benefits of
Family Involvement

Susan was sure to be a basketball star. Everyone knew she would break records and play with a professional basketball team one day. She made the varsity team as a seventh grade middle school student. In high school, she was an unstoppable point guard and led her team to many state championships. She attended a college of distinction on full athletic scholarship, though she could have gone with an academic scholarship. In college, she commanded the crowds' attention. She became a card-carrying member of one of the WNBA teams. As remarkable as her skills were, I found the support of her parents more striking. They missed not one home or away game while she played in secondary school or college. One parent participated in most events at the school and volunteered for several functions. They attended PTO meetings and sat in parent conferences with teachers to track her academic progress.

Her parents support and involvement benefited the student, her parents, her teachers, and the school. She earned higher test scores and grades and gained admission to a prestigious university. I imagine her accomplishments on the basketball court and the classroom gave her high self-esteem.

Her parents benefited by not having to pay for college. Her teachers benefited because they had her parents' support and could help her reach her full potential, a source of pride and a morale booster. The school benefited because her SAT scores were high and helped the school maintain its satisfactory status, as well as the attention that resulted from her accomplishments.

When parents are involved, students, parents, teachers, and schools benefit. Some of the benefits are higher graduation rates, college admission, higher student achievement, higher student self-esteem, better school-home relationships, and improved teacher morale.

Teacher Attributes Related to Successful Parental Involvement

Over the past ten years, I have worked with thousands of teachers, administrators, principals, and counselors. One beneficial activity I do with them is ask them to think about the greatest teacher they ever had and list the attributes that made that teacher great. I like the activity because it lets educators reflect on how great teachers behave and interact with students. Some of their responses include *warmth, openness, flexibility, reliability, accessibility, supportive attitude, responsiveness, readiness to listen,* and *positive attitudes.*

If the workshop's focus is parental involvement, I also ask them to close their eyes and recall how that great teacher interacted with their parents. Many educators recall times when a teacher called their parents to report on their progress. Others remember when a great teacher took them home to talk with their parents after a bad day in school. Others tell how a teacher regularly wrote note to parents. Some recalled a great teacher calling to remind their parents of meetings or school events. Many said a great teacher stayed positive, even when students failed tests: "He made an F, but he can do better if he studies."

Then I asked what their parents did and said: *spanked me, thanked the teacher for calling, took me to class the next day and stayed, gave me a treat, hugged me, made me study for hours, called the teacher the next day to find out how I behaved, baked the teacher some cookies, sent that great teacher a Christmas present.*

Comments like those about a great teacher's attributes lead me to conclude a positive attitude, sensitivity to parents, respect for parents, genuine interest in children, and effective communication skills are signs of a great teacher. You can be among the great educators who encourage parents to be involved with their children's education.

Summary

Educators can involve parents meaningfully when they are aware of the personal assumptions, beliefs, and prejudices that can affect relationships with families. Reflecting on and examining assumptions, beliefs, and prejudices helps educators discover their negative feelings and perceptions of parents. Educators can also develop plans for involving parents when they know the barriers many parents face. Specific teacher attributes have a positive effect on efforts to involve parents. Educators with them can involve parents in a variety of school activities.

Part Two
Strategies for Involving Parents

When my second child was in fifth grade, his teacher needed a sweet potato to conduct an experiment. She sent parents a letter explaining the experiment and requesting a homegrown sweet potato, among other items. She pointed out that a sweet potato store bought would not suit the experiment. I volunteered to provide the sweet potato. We did not have a homegrown sweet potato, but my mother—who lived 185 miles way—did. The weekend after the teacher sent the letter home, we drove to Grandma's house for a homegrown sweet potato.

My child's teacher invited parents to participate in an experiment she was doing with students. I decided to supply the sweet potato, and parents provided the other things her letter asked for. Sending home a letter asking parents for help gave all the parents a chance to be involved and select from a menu of items to contribute.

I define strategy as various approaches to involve parents in their children's education meaningfully. Some are:

- strategies for improving communication between parents and teachers;
- strategies to involve parents from various ethnic and socio-economic backgrounds;
- strategies to assist with defensive, hostile, and frustrated parents;

- strategies to build relationships with families;
- strategies to build relationships with students;
- strategies for effective parent-teacher conferences;
- strategies for involving parents in School-To-Work Programs.

Strategies for Improving Communication with Parents

Use strategies to improve communication, since ineffective communication affects parental involvement negatively. Educators who use strategies to improve communication are likely to increase parental involvement with the students they teach.

1. *Communicate effectively.* Most parents I work with as a teacher and counselor like teachers to contact them frequently using a variety of methods. Many prefer phone calls. Others, due to work schedules, appreciate notes or newsletters. Some with internet access prefer e-mail. Parents feel better about the school when they have communication from teachers and the school.

2. *Communicate respectfully.* Educational jargon often frustrates parents and leaves them with unanswered questions. Language should be clear and simple. Written communication to parents should be free of language they likely do not understand.

3. *Generalizations do not work.* Parents inside ethnic groups do not necessarily communicate the same way. Educators must communicate with

parents based on identified communication practices.

4. *Engaged listening.* Use listening skills that communicate caring and attentiveness. I learned techniques that demonstrate good listening in the counselor education program. My professors told me that if I kept eye contact, listened for feelings, rephrased and repeated, did not interrupt, gave appropriate feedback, and asked open ended questions, I would be a good listener. Those strategies have worked for me most of the time for years. Many people say I am a good listener. The one thing that works all the time, however, is to remember that I could be the one who needs someone to listen.

5. *Body language speaks.* My mother knew when I was lying. How? She watched my body language. I know when my children are telling the truth or when they are conveniently leaving certain information out. Sometimes they yawn before they speak. Other times they cast their eyes down just before they speak. Or they cough or respond angrily or shuffle their feet. Therefore, no matter what I told my mother or what my children say to me, my mother watched and I pay close attention to body language. Parents also analyze educator's body language to decide if they are genuine.

Educators must be careful to send a congruent message to parents through words and body language. They evaluate facial expressions for respect and acceptance. Parents look for enthusiasm, confidence, and interest in educators' posture and eye contact. Parents generally like educators who respect personal space without seeming distant and aloof.

6. *Contact information.* Many educators prefer face-to-face conferences as do some parents. Other parents prefer phone conferences, which should not be read as lack of initiative or interest. Perhaps culture is involved. Just remember that the goal is parental involvement however parents find it most appealing.

Strategies to involve parents in the classroom

Invite parents to participate in the classroom actively, a great additional support for teachers that shows students their parents can be involved beyond meetings or joining a parents' organization. Inviting parents into the classroom is a way to help parents understand the teacher's job and the importance of their support.

Among strategies for involving parents in the classroom are:

1. *Give parents guidance.* Generate a list of important items parents should do or discuss with their children at home. Some parents are challenged readers, and teachers can help them by keeping written communications short, concise, and in list form when possible. The list can include:

   - class rules
   - school rules
   - specific content
   - study guides
   - class goals
   - class beliefs

2. *Classroom Visits.* Inviting parents into the classroom as observers or volunteers increases parents' trust for teachers and makes them feel welcome. Visiting the classroom gives parents a chance to be actively involved.

3. *Parent participation at home.* Tailor some assignment to encourage parent-student collaboration. When parents work with their children, they feel they are contributing to their academic success. Parents should understand, however, that if they do a child's assignment, the student loses the opportunity to learn skills the assignment is designed to teach.

4. *Make home visits if possible.* Many educators live outside the community where their students live, which makes it harder for parents to get to know them. Some educators drive a long way and may not be able to attend after school events or schedule conferences in the afternoon. Home visits are one way educators can meet parents and involve them in their children's education. Homes visit are effective means of involving parents.

5. *Parents' gifts and talents in the classroom.* Many parents have a gift or talent to share with students. Teachers can identify something they need in the class and solicit help from parents. Parents can build things or paint the

classroom. Parents can also be guest speakers or special guests for a specific activity. Try to find ways to encourage parents to bring their talents and gifts into the classroom. Making meaningful contributions gives parents a sense of pride and empowerment.

6. *Personal invitation.* Personally invite parents to attend and support other children in activities— concerts, plays, athletic events, musicals. That may take a little more time out of your day, but think of the benefits:

- supportive parents
- higher student achievement
- less behavior problems
- more parental involvement

7. *Seek parents' assistance with specific activities that involve students.* Involved parents are more likely to understand and support a teacher's goals and practices. Offer parents a variety of activities from which to choose. Perhaps a parent cannot help in the class or in the school but can provide a service. Any involvement is positive. Parents know how they could best get involved in the classroom. Too often teachers assume parents want to be involved only in certain ways.

8. *Understand culture.* The American classroom is becoming increasingly culturally and ethnically diverse, a fact that requires teachers learn about and try to understand their students' parents' cultures and ethnic backgrounds.

9. *Always make parents feel welcome and comfortable, since they have a right to be there.* Many parents are uncomfortable in the school environment. Some, because they did not have much success in school. Others, because they are not well educated and shy away from situations with others where they might have trouble communicating. Yet others, because of bad experiences with school personnel. Whatever the reason, teachers must do their best to make parents feel comfortable and welcome.

Strategies for Effective Parent Conferences

Parent conferences are a time for sharing and listening. Educators can share useful information with parents about academic, social, and behavioral progress. Parents in turn are a rich source of information about children's habits, likes, dislikes, and temperament. A conference is among the best ways to involve parents and to build relationships between schools and homes. Here are ways to make conferences as effective, as informative, and non-threatening as possible.

Before the conference:

- *Contact parents well before a conference.* Inform parents why you think a conference is desirable or needed. If parents request a conference, meet them as soon as you can.
- *Send a personal note outlining the agenda.* A phone call does as well. Often a phone call becomes the conference and makes a face-to-face meeting unnecessary.
- *Encourage parents to generate lists of questions for you.* In a meeting, parents often forget what they want to ask. Writing questions down assures they get answers.

- *Prepare a conference folder.* The folder should contain positive examples of work and evidence of skills students need to improve.
- *Arrange a comfortable private area with adult chairs.* Making parents comfortable puts them at ease.

During the conference:

1. *Meet with parents alone.* Unless you believe parents will be difficult to work with, meet with them alone. Uninvited school personnel at meetings do not help and may intimidate or anger parents. If you are uncomfortable meeting without a third party, ask the parents' permission to record the conference or tell them in advance that a third party will be present.

2. *Establish rapport quickly.* Ask parents something about their work or about their interests.

3. *Understand parents as advocates for their children.* Do not interpret parental advocacy as belligerence or criticism. Do not take offense if parents defend their children. Teachers must:

    - give parents an opportunity to voice concerns fully;
    - respond honestly and sensitively to parents' concerns;

- make suggestions for improvement;
- avoid arguments.

4. *Emphasize the positive.* Comment on a student's unique gifts and talents. Research suggests parents use teachers' knowledge of children's personalities and interests as a screening device and are more willing to listen to deal with problems if they see teachers care enough to notice their child's special qualities. A positive story about their child can set the stage for a successful conference.

5. *Avoid overloading parents.* Pick one or two areas students need to improve. Some parents feel overwhelmed if they have to address many concerns in one meeting.

6. *Learn from parents.* Involve parents in generating solutions to solve problems. Devote at least half the conference to parents' concerns, ideas, and questions.

7. *Close the conference with action steps:*

- give parents specific times and numbers where you can be reached;
- develop a plan for parent-teacher collaboration;
- provide resources and materials, if appropriate, to address the matters at issue;
- agree to meet again if necessary.

8. *Know school and class policies, and stick to them.* Parents trust teachers who know and follow policies. If a parent asks for something against a class or school policy, explain the policy briefly. Teachers can also offer alternatives in line with policy or practice to meet parents' requests.

9. *Stick with facts and avoid making subjective comments.* Comment on what children do, how they can improve, and how you want to help. Discuss facts (*i.e.* performance, standardized test scores, test grades, daily participation, homework) that can be substantiated with data.

After the conference:

- Make brief notes about the conference.
- Follow through with plans made to address parents' concerns.
- Respond to suggestions made and questions raised at the conference.
- Follow-up with a written note to the parents that outlines the concerns raised and the solutions agreed upon at the conference.
- Keep parents informed of steps taken since the conference. Consult with the principal if necessary.

Strategies for Building Relationships with Parents

Building positive relationships with parents is critical if educators hope to work with them effectively. Nothing fits better here than the educator's golden rule: "Do unto parents as you would have them do unto your children." Simple but powerful. Ask yourself these questions:

- How would you like your children's teacher to respond to you?
- Would you like your children's teacher to be sensitive to your culture?
- Would you like your children's teacher to communicate with you regularly?
- Would you like your children's teacher to respect you as an equal partner in educating your children?
- Would you like to hear from your children's teacher only when they are in trouble?

Strategies for Dealing with Defensive, Hostile, or or Frustrated Parents

Managing a situation with defensive, hostile, or frustrated parents can be unsettling, particularly for inexperienced educators. Parents who yell or make accusations and demands, can be overwhelming and inhibit parental involvement efforts. I recall the first time an irate parent confronted me. In my third year as a teacher, a mother called me for a conference. Her high-pitched voice on the phone told me she was upset. She insisted on seeing me immediately. When I asked if something was wrong, she said she would tell me when she came to the school. I agreed to see her that afternoon after students were dismissed. She arrived about thirty minutes before the end of the school day. The secretary came to tell me she was waiting in the main office. The bell rang, and I took the children to the bus area and made sure they were securely seated. I returned to the main office and invited the mother to follow me to my classroom. When we got there, I sat down and so did she. I opened by asking the reason for her visit. She said she was upset because her child was not allowed to play with her friends the day before. She accused me of being insensitive and mean to children and demanded an explanation. I listened until she finished. I told her I was glad to see her and then gave her the explanation she demanded. I made it clear that her child used profanity with his friends the day before and that was why he was not permitted to play. Students who swear lost one or more privileges. She calmed down, apologized to me, and vowed to "get him good" when she got home.

Most educators eventually face angry or dissatisfied parents. When that happens, I suggest the following ways to help the parents relax so meaningful conversation can take place:

1. *Use engaged listening.* Let parents voice opinions and concerns without interruption. Take notes about concerns to address later. Maintain eye contact and good posture. Acknowledge with an occasional nod of your head and make "I see" statements. *I see you are upset . . . , I see what you are saying . . . , I see you care about your child and his progress.*

2. *Listen for feelings behind words.* Validate parent's feelings by acknowledging, nodding the head, or other gestures that indicate understanding. Try to ascertain if parents are frustrated, angry, hopeless, or afraid. Acknowledging feelings shows understanding.

3. *Ask for clarification.* If parents make statements that need further clarification

for an appropriate response, ask for it. Ask open-ended, focused questions to get as much information as possible.

4. *Respond to parents' concerns non-defensively.* Parents are their children's advocates. Do not take it personally. Remember the parents' culture and respond in ways that show sensitivity to that culture.

5. *Start with a positive statement about the parents' concern.* When your turn to speak comes, start with positive statements about the parents. For example, *I am pleased you are here* or *I appreciate your concern for your children's success.*

6. *Respond with facts and observed behavior.* State the facts and support them with data. If grades are the problem, explain how grades are determined and why a student did not make the grade his parents anticipated. The student could have missed assignments or failed to complete a project.

7. *Outline your policies and procedures.* That helps parents understand policies and procedures and why they exist. Provide copies of policies and procedures if needed or requested.

8. *Remember, a teacher conference has two goals.* Helping parents get involved and offering suggestions to help their children are the conference's two major goals. Emphasize

student strengths and offer suggestions for improvement.

9. *Parents are often frustrated and confused.* Parents are frustrated when their children do not succeed and confused because they know their children can perform well. Explain what their children can do to improve grades or behavior. That transfers responsibility to the students, and parents feel good when their children get another chance.

10. *Address accusations immediately.* If parents make unfounded accusations, involve an administrator immediately. If possible, escort the parent to the administrators to voice their concerns. Take accusations seriously and handle them at once.

11. *Ask parent for suggestions for solving problems.* Once the parents calm down, ask for suggestions to resolve problems. Make note if their suggestions require authorization from third parties or if you need more information before you can answer. Let parents know when they can expect a response.

12. *Look for areas of agreement.* Discuss points on which both parties agree. For example, both teachers and parents want students to do well and reach their full potential. Find areas of agreement, and parents become far more cooperative.

13. *Stay calm.* Managing uncomfortable situations with angry parents requires composure. An aggressive, angry, or defensive response only exacerbates matters and escalates tension. Stay calm.

14. *Look for a win-win solution.* Parents want to know their concerns are taken seriously, and they want a solution that favors their children. That may be possible if the remedy does not conflict with school policy or rules. When there is a conflict, consider options with the broadest latitude. For example, if students fail to complete a project by the deadline and earn zero for a grade, teachers could let them turn it in for a maximum possible grade of 75.

Strategies for Involving Parents in School-to-Work Activities

School-to-work activities prepare students for work or for other post-secondary opportunities. They include job shadowing, apprenticeship, internships, and mentoring. Parent support of school-to-work activities provides a variety of options for students. Parents who participate and encourage their children to participate in school-to-work activities find their children exit high school with skills and knowledge they do not ordinarily acquire in the classroom. Educators can encourage and invite parents to:

- Share their jobs, occupations, and/or professions with the class;
- work with teachers to plan career awareness and career exploration activities;
- assist with refreshments at school wide School-To-Work activities;
- receive interpretation of career inventories along with students;
- read career inventories at home with a detailed explanation of results;
- serve as career mentors for students;
- provide apprenticeship and shadowing opportunities for students;

- offer full or part-time employment for students whose interest and ability match the parent's business;
- assist with the upkeep and update of an Opportunity Board designed to keep parents and students abreast of careers, jobs, apprenticeships, and shadowing opportunities;
- design a career bulletin board;
- read stories about various careers to a class;
- visit with the School-To-Work coordinator and/or career counselor to discuss career and School-To-Work opportunities;
- participate or visit during all in class School-To-Work activities;
- take one or more of the career inventories students take to understanding the inventories better;
- organize a School-To-Work activity for a class or a school;
- publish a yearly School-To-Work calendar for parents showing activities scheduled for a class or a school;
- provide a School-To-Work booth or classroom parents can visit for information at every open house;
- publish a parent volunteer yearbook and give a copy to every parent who volunteers to assist with School-To-Work activities;

- set up a parent center at school with a variety of career materials and information about School-To-Work opportunities parents can check out and use at home.
- publish a monthly School-To-Work newsletter;
- create a "Parent Hall of Fame" bulletin board to highlight parent careers of children in a class or a school;
- offer School-To-Work seminars and workshops for parents at school;
- offer School-To-Work seminars and workshops for parents at community centers and churches.

Strategies for Involving Parents in School-Wide Programs

A school-wide program is a prime opportunity to involve parents where they can participate in many ways, either lending support or participating actively. School-wide activities require teamwork to be successful. Parents can contribute time, talent, and expertise. Some school-wide activities are:

- stage assistance at musical programs;
- service on the school improvement council;
- speaking at career days;
- judging art shows;
- speaking during drug awareness week;
- donating goods and services to the prom;
- managing the concession stand at athletic events;
- chair a fund drive;
- helping with school beautification;
- selling tickets at athletic or fine arts events;
- calling to remind parents of specific events.
-

Strategies for Using Technology to Involve Parents

It is three o'clock in the afternoon. The phone rings. The parent expects to hear someone answer, Hello. She repeats her greeting and holds the phone a few seconds, waiting for a voice. The a pre-recorded message begins. "*Hello, this is Mr. Carol of High Pine High School. This message is to remind parents of the parent conference night tomorrow, Tuesday, February 5, 2006. The conferences will begin at 6:30 P.M. Parents will have the opportunity to speak with teachers and counselors about course selection for their children next year. If you have questions about tomorrow night, please call the school. Thank you and have a good day.*"

The principal sent an automated message to all parents whose children attended High Pine, using a program called Phone–Link: technology at work. Use technology to involve parents by informing them of upcoming events and activities and providing access to information about their students. Automated messages are a good tool to get a message to all parents.

Some schools have software that lets parents track their children's progress on-line. With an access code and a mouse click, parents can view academic history, discipline, attendance, and review transcripts to determine grades earned in each course, number of credits completed toward graduation, grade point averages, and class rank. Discipline records reveal if their children were referred to the principal and the consequences applied. Parents concerned about their children skipping school or cutting class can log on to determine the time and date of absences. Tracking their students' progress is important to parents. The Internet makes it easier and more convenient.

Many schools have elaborate websites that provide information about policy and procedures, curriculum, links to other relevant websites such as collegeboard.com, dates and hours of athletic events, faculty and staff lists with e-mail addresses and numbers for voice mail. Staff members have web pages on many of them and post syllabi, assignments, samples, information on scholarships, newsletters, and required materials. Posting information on websites can keep parents informed.

As technology advances, other modes of communicating with parents become available, such as cell phones for texting messages to parents. Electronic message boards in prominent places in and outside buildings can give parents vital information, congratulate students, or to announce upcoming events.

Strategies for Community Outreach

Community outreach programs to increase parental involvement give educators a chance to make personal contact with parents they would not otherwise meet. Some parents are more comfortable meeting educators in familiar places, like community centers, churches, and community leaders' homes, where they can relax and be themselves. Parents are likelier to ask questions and voice opinions if they feel safe.

I organized a community parental involvement program several years ago for parents of students at the school where I worked. Parental involvement at the school was already strong, with many parents volunteering for a variety of tasks. Parents supported academic and athletic booster clubs, attended open houses and other school wide functions. Parent-teacher conferences averaged ten per week. Most of the involved parents represented one segment of the population: they were middle to high level economically, and most had college degrees. Parents from low socioeconomic backgrounds or parents without college degrees were less visible. We started the Parental Involvement Coalition to create and maintain a connection between those parents and the school.

We contacted pastors of churches and managers of community centers and hired a coordinator with grant funds from the state Department of Education's Safe School Office. The coordinator explained the program to the pastors and others, and they joined the coalition enthusiastically. They agreed to host at least one meeting apiece. Meetings with parents were then scheduled monthly on a rotating basis at area churches and community centers to discuss issues, learn, and ask questions. The hosts provided refreshments. Each pastor appointed a parent representative to attend all the meetings to gather information for other church members which the pastors let them share on Sunday mornings. Pastors and community center leaders provided the space and support that made the program a success.

The following elements ensured the Parental Involvement Coalition's success.

1. A detailed description of the program with goals, budget, funding, personnel, location, agencies, timeline, calendar, and format.
2. A state funded grant.
3. The coordinator trained in organizing and conducting meetings and aware of best practices for working with pastors and community center managers.
4. Involved pastors and community center managers.

5. A calendar (developed by the coordinator) showing location, date, and time of each meeting.

6. A partnership agreement between the school, pastors, and community center managers, stipulating the responsibilities of all participants.

7. Organizational meetings.

8. A parent pre-survey at the initial meeting to determine topics of interest and benefit to parents.

9. All scheduled meetings occurred on time.

10. A post-survey among parents to determine the program's effectiveness.

The Parental Involvement Coalition is one example of how schools can connect with parents in the community. Schools must develop creative ways to keep parents informed and involved in their children's education. Student academic achievement increases as parents become more involved.

Summary

Parental involvement efforts require a variety of approaches appropriate for parents from various ethnic and socio-economic backgrounds. Strategies to improve communication, build relationships, manage hostile parents, conduct effective parent-teacher conferences, and support school-to-work activities can improve parental involvement. Technology can help educators involve parents. Educators using those strategies often enjoy a pleasant relationship with parents, and parents' trust and support of teachers increase.

Part Three
Implementation

"What does your school do to increase parental involvement", one participant asked another.

"Well, I don't know if we do anything specific to involve parents. We do have open house, but only one third of the parents attend. What does your school do?"

"That's why I'm here. We have open house, and we invite parents to meet with teachers but have few takers. I'm here to find out about strategies other educators have used successfully to increase parental involvement."

"So am I."

I overheard that conversation at a conference I attended on parental involvement. Educators are aware of the status of parental involvement at their schools or in the classroom. Recognizing the problem is the beginning, and taking steps to increase parental involvement can make the difference. Implementing strategies can increase parent attendance at key activities and encourage involvement in other ways.

Implementation is *using* strategies to increase parental involvement. Strategies are effective only if we use them. Implementation requires the collaborative effort of many school personnel. Implementing strategies involves time, flexibility, and familiarity with the strategies.

Time. Educators must spend time determining appropriate strategies to use for each student in the school. Selecting strategies appropriate for parents is more likely to increase parental involvement than some "one size fits all" model.

Flexibility. Educators must be flexible about the types of parental involve opportunities they offer parents. Some parents may attend open houses, while others prefer to donate goods and services.

Familiarity with Strategies. Educators will use only strategies they know about and understand. Consulting with colleagues and conducting research can yield a variety of strategies from which to choose.

Summary

Time, flexibility, and familiarity with strategies will help educators increase parental involvement. Effective implementation of parental involvement initiatives requires the collaboration of many school personnel.

Part Four
Assessing Parental Involvement

When a school where I worked hosted open house, we recorded the number of parents attending as one indicator of how involved parents were. We also considered the quantity of parents visiting the school counseling office, number of volunteers, amount of parent-teacher conferences, and membership in parent organizations. Those are important indicators that helped us verify how many parents were involved in easily tracked, up-front activities. What about less apparent activities?

The question is, what must parents do to qualify as *involved?* They can be involved in numerous ways. When parents send their children to school well groomed and fed, you can call that parental involvement. They took the time to be sure their children got to school without worrying about food or being teased by other students because they were dirty. Educators can say parents are involved when parents monitor homework to be sure their children complete homework assignments. Parents calling the school to review attendance records is parental involvement, as is reading and signing information and returning it to school on time. Parents who encourage their children to do their best in school are involved parents. All those and others acts of parents show parental involvement.

Some educators fail to see other actions as parental involvement. Although, If schools evaluated both traditional and non-traditional forms of parental involvement, schools would realize increased levels of parental involvement immediately.

Non-traditional forms of parental involvement take time to assess. Educators must record recurrences of easily observed behaviors, such as how a student is dressed. They must devise ways to assess less obvious or apparent parent behavior, such as encouraging children to work hard in school. A parent survey can help discover the information. Not all non-traditional parental involvement activities may be susceptible to adequate assessment. For the moment, just knowing that non-traditional forms of parental involvement exist may be enough to spark discussion among educators to help them appreciate the many different ways parents can be involved in their children's education.

Summary

Traditional and non-traditional forms of parental involvement have a positive impact on student achievement. Educators would gain a more realistic picture of the extent in which parents are involved if they assess both.

Conclusion

Awareness, strategies, implementation, and assessment all play a role in increasing parental involvement. Educators with pre-service and in-service training on involving parents have the information they need to work with parents from various ethnic and socioeconomic backgrounds. Knowledge about a variety of strategies to increase parental involvement can foster an appropriate match of strategies to parents. Implementation of those strategies enhances or increases parental involvement in an assortment of activities. An assessment of traditional and non-traditional parental involvement activities profoundly affects a school's parental involvement status. Awareness, strategies, implementation, and assessment are key factors in increasing parental involvement at a school or in classrooms.

APPENDIX

Parental Involvement Checklist

Directions: Use this checklist to identify how, when, and where parents are involved and to gauge the level of parental involvement in the school or classroom. This checklist can also help educators determine areas where parental involvement initiatives need to be implemented or improved.

Check the box in the column beside each activity and record the date the activity was conducted. Location, parent response, and comments can also be recorded to provide additional information.

🕐	Date	Activity	Parent Response	Comments
		Parent volunteers in class		
		Parent supports teachers when children need discipline		
		Parent brings or sends children to school on time		
		Parent volunteers at school		
		Parent contacted by phone		
		Parent contacted by mail		
		Parent contacted by e-mail		
		Parent newsletter mailed or sent home		
		Parent notified of important dates		
		Parent visited in the home		
		Parent used as expert in class or school		
		Parent invited to specific events		
		Parent conferences conducted for each student		
		Parent provided with progress report		

⏱	Date	Activity	Parent Response	Comments
		Parent provided with report cards		
		Parent can access information on the school website and teacher web page		
		Parent knows how to contact school		
		Parent knows how to contact teacher		
		Parents knows how to contact counselor		
		Parent knows how to contact administration		
		Parent praised for involvement		
		Parent's initial contact is positive		
		Parent sends children to school prepared		
		Parent sends children to school wearing clean clothes		
		Parent calls school to check on children		
		Parent responds to requests for help		
		Parent teaches children acceptable behaviors		

Made in the USA
San Bernardino, CA
18 March 2013